JULIE KRONE

A Winning Jockey

by Dorothy Callahan

Taking part BOOKS

dP DILLON PRESS, INC.
Minneapolis, Minnesota 55415

Photographic Acknowledgments

Photos have been reproduced through the courtesy of Lisa Kryston; Bob Coglianese/New York Racing Association; Bill Denver, Don Brown/Winners Photo; Churchill Downs; Monmouth Park; Dave Rentas/*The Post*; Michael Sargeant/White House; and Breeders' Cup Limited.

Library of Congress Cataloging-in-Publication Data

Callahan, Dorothy. M.

   Julie Krone, a winning jockey / Dorothy Callahan.

     p.   cm. — (Taking part books)

   Summary: Discusses the childhood, education, early riding career, major races, records, titles, views, and personal life of jockey Julie Krone.

   ISBN 0-87518-425-1 (lib. bdg.) : $9.95

   1. Krone, Julie—Juvenile literature.   2. Jockeys—United States—Juvenile literature. 3. Women jockeys—United States—Juvenile literature. [1. Krone, Julie. 2. Jockeys.] I. Title.

SF336.K76C35   1990

798.4'0092—dc20

[B]

[92]   89-26061

                                       CIP

                                     AC

Dillon Press, Inc., 242 Portland Avenue South
Minneapolis, Minnesota 55415

Printed in the United States of America
1 2 3 4 5 6 7 8 9 10 99 98 97 96 95 94 93 92 91 90

About the Author

An experienced writer, Dorothy Callahan has authored four children's books, two of which have focused on the sport of horse racing. Her numerous articles have appeared in *Scholastic Scope, Ranger Rick, Thoroughbred Record,* and *American Turf Monthly,* to name a few. Ms. Callahan currently lives in New Jersey, where she is a learning consultant for learning disabled students, as well as a teacher of gifted and talented students.

CONTENTS

JULIE KRONE

Horses were all Julie Krone thought about when she was growing up on a Michigan farm. Today, she is one of the world's best jockeys.

Julie learned to ride from her mother, Judi Krone, a precision rider and horse trainer. Judi trusted her daughter to ride a few miles away from home even before she was old enough to start school.

Julie was five years old when she won her first ribbon in a horse show. As she grew, she won prizes in contests all over Michigan. She knew in her first horse race, though, that she wanted to be a jockey.

At the age of seventeen, Julie entered the world of thoroughbred racing. Her early years were spent proving to male jockeys and trainers that she was good. She won races at tracks in Florida, Maryland, Delaware, and Pennsylvania before moving to the "major league" tracks in New Jersey and New York.

By the time she turned 25, Julie Krone was the leading female jockey in the world. Today, she has won nearly 2,000 races, and has captured the "best jockey" titles at three race tracks. Today, her goal is simple—to be *the* best jockey in the world.

I can do anything with a horse

It was late on an autumn evening in 1989. The crowd at The Meadowlands racetrack in New Jersey cheered as the pack of horses sped down the stretch. Riding the leading horse, *Foresta*, was a four-foot, ten-inch jockey named Julie Krone. When her horse crossed the finish line in front, the cheering became louder. She had just become the first jockey in the track's history to win six races in one day.

For Julie Krone, it was just one more record set on the way to becoming the leading female jockey in the world.

Julieann Louise Krone was born in Benton Harbor, Michigan, on July 24, 1963. Her riding career began on her father's back. She soon moved from

Donald Krone to her dog Twiggy, then to Dixie, the Shetland pony.

"I don't remember a time when I didn't ride," Julie says in her high-pitched voice. "It was just natural to me to be on a horse's back."

It was natural to her mother, Judi, too. One day when Julie was two years old, a woman came to look at a horse she was thinking of buying from the Krones.

"Look how gentle he is," Judi said to the woman. Without thinking, she lifted Julie onto the horse's back. As he trotted off, Judi realized what she had done. She watched nervously as little Julie reached down, grabbed the horse's reins, and turned the horse back to her mother.

Julie was four years old when her parents bought a ten-acre farm in Eau Claire, Michigan. For the Krones, it was the perfect place to live.

Julie remembers to thank her mount, Some Romance, *on her way to the winner's circle.*

For Julie and her brother, Donnie, who was three years older, the farm meant pets—and lots of them. Sometimes there were dogs, cats, chickens, rabbits, turtles, gerbils, toads, and even a goat parading in and out of the house.

One day, Julie even brought her horse into the

dining room. She had been having trouble getting the saddle on, so she led him into the house to have her mother help her. Judi Krone wanted her daughter to be independent. Together, they rigged up a pulley in one of the trees that Julie could use to lift the saddle off the ground and onto the horse's back.

Judi also taught Julie to be patient and understanding of all animals. As she was teaching Julie to ride, Judi would say, "You can't make him [the horse] do what he doesn't want to do. Think about what's on his mind, then encourage him to do his best." It was a lesson Julie would never forget.

If Julie fell off the horse during a lesson, Judi lifted her right back on. "If you're afraid," she said, "the horse will know it."

By the time she was six years old, Julie was allowed to ride several miles away from home on her own. "Nothing taught me better horsemanship," she remembers, "than falling off and having to walk back three miles."

When Julie wasn't on a horse's back, she played ball, climbed trees, or went fishing with her brother and the neighborhood boys. Sometimes, Julie harnessed her Great Dane, Arrow, to the front of her sled in the wintertime and pretended he was a horse.

Summertime meant freedom for Julie. She didn't like school and homework, because they took her away from her horses. Although she wasn't very successful in school, Julie was a star in the show ring. She had won her first horse show prize by the age of five. Every summer after that, Julie and Judi Krone traveled throughout Michigan to compete in horse shows. By September of each year, Julie's wall was full of ribbons for trail riding, show jumping, and dressage.

When Julie was fifteen years old, life became suddenly serious. Her parents decided to get a divorce. Julie wrote sad poems about it and spent a lot of time riding her horses alone. After the divorce, her brother, Donnie, chose to live with Donald Krone. Judi and Julie were left by themselves on the farm with the animals. They became even closer to each other than they had been in the past.

In 1979, Julie persuaded her mother to spend the spring break from school at Churchill Downs, home of the Kentucky Derby. Julie had decided years before that she wanted to become a jockey, and she wanted to show her mother what life at a racetrack was like.

In April, Judi Krone drove the family camper to the racetrack in Louisville, Kentucky. Once there, Judi found a job almost right away. She forced Julie to go off on her own, saying, "Nobody will hire a kid who looks ten years old if their momma is with them."

Wandering around the stables, Julie met Clarence and Donna Picou. Clarence had been a leading jockey when he was younger. Now he trained horses. When he asked Julie what she could do, she said, "I can do anything with a horse—ride, brush, groom—you name it." Clarence agreed to hire her, and by the end of the week, Julie had convinced the Picous to let her work for them during the summer vacation.

Back in Eau Claire, Julie felt as if it took longer than six weeks for June to arrive. But soon, she was traveling to Louisville and Churchill Downs again.

Once there, she tried to convince Clarence to let her become a morning workout rider. She had been watching her hero, eighteen-year-old Steve Cauthen,

Churchill Downs racetrack, home of the Kentucky Derby, where Julie got her start in thoroughbred racing.

ride on television. He had won the Kentucky Derby in 1978, and Julie tried to imitate his riding style—head down, seat up, back level.

When Clarence finally gave Julie the chance to be a workout rider, she almost lost it. Taking a horse out on the track, Julie began to daydream about the Kentucky Derby. She let the horse run much too fast, making Clarence very angry.

"If you want to be a jockey, young lady, you had better listen to the trainer," he warned. Julie was learning that it took more than good horsemanship to be a jockey.

In October, Judi Krone came to pick up Julie and take her back to Michigan. But Julie's mind was on the racetrack, and school did not go well for her. Many girls Julie's age were wearing makeup and going on dates. Julie was more interested in becoming a better rider.

Julie rode her first winners on the Michigan Fair tracks. Here she poses after placing first with Hurricane Hatti.

That winter, Julie practiced her riding nearly every day. Even when snow was on the ground, she and her Arabian horse, Ralph, galloped in the plowed section of the dirt along the road. At night, she wrote about her progress in her diary. "I know I can be the greatest jockey in the world!" she wrote.

It didn't matter to Julie that the first female jockey had been given a license only ten years before, or that many trainers would not let a woman ride their horses.

In June, Julie Krone got her start as a jockey. Some friends of the family had an Arabian horse that they raced at fairgrounds during the summer. Julie was to be their jockey. On July 4, 1980, the trainer led Julie and her mount into the starting gate at the Lake Odessa fairgrounds. He told her, "If you fall off, you won't get stepped on. This horse will be last."

But Julie wanted to prove the trainer wrong. She started the race in seventh place, but moved up quickly, finishing second. In the stands, Judi Krone watched. She was very proud of Julie's skill. Although it made her sad, she said later she knew that Julie had taken her first step away from home.

Julie likes to get to know the horses she will ride. Here, she walks a possible winner around the stable area.

I'm going to be a jockey

The three months Julie spent on the Michigan Fair racing circuit made her sure of one thing. She wanted to begin her riding career right away.

Back in the classroom again, Julie was unhappy. She felt even more out of place among her classmates, and could not concentrate on her schoolwork. Finally, she told her mother that she wanted to leave school. At seventeen, many jockeys had already been riding for a year.

Judi was worried about Julie dropping out of school and living on her own at such a young age. But Julie promised to get her high school diploma later. Remembering her own dreams at the age of seventeen, Judi agreed to let Julie live with her grandparents in Tampa, Florida. Julie would be able to look for work at the Tampa Bay Downs racetrack.

In December 1980, mother and daughter arrived in Florida. They had not even unpacked before Julie dragged Judi off to the racetrack with her. There, they met Jerry Pace, a horse trainer.

"So, you want to be a jockey," Jerry Pace said, smiling.

"No," Julie answered. "I'm *going* to be a jockey."

Although he wasn't sure if such a tiny girl had any ability, Jerry boosted Julie onto a horse. He told her to jog the horse up to the half-mile pole, then let him run hard to the finish line.

The horse took off, snorting and bobbing its head, while Julie searched for the half-mile marker. She couldn't find it. Finally, she shouted to a passing rider, who pointed to a red and white striped pole in the distance.

When Julie brought the horse in from the track, Jerry Pace asked her how the ride had been. As if she had not had any doubt about what she was doing, Julie told him, "Nothing I can't handle." She got the job. That night, though, she drew a careful map of the track and all the distance markers, and pasted it to the ceiling of her bedroom.

By the fifth morning at the Tampa racetrack, Julie was able to get her jockey's license. Although she was still worried about Julie, Judi Krone went back to Michigan.

Arriving at the racetrack before sunup each day, Julie exercised Jerry's horses and waited for a chance to race. On January 30, 1981, she finally got it.

Putting on the jockey's white pants with her name sewn in the back made her feel like a real jockey at last. Then she put on the nylon shirt, called racing silks, in the horse owner's colors, and

Julie likes to take a horse on the track for a morning workout before she rides it in a race.

walked out to the track. She rode a horse called *Tiny Star*, just missing first place.

Julie did not yet have an agent, someone to get mounts for her from the trainers. Instead, she hung around the barns of Jerry Pace's friends, trying to get work.

One of these trainers let her ride *Lord Farkle*, an older horse that had been racing for several years. Julie surprised everyone when she brought him across the finish line first. She came in first in three of her next six races, and then won on *Lord Farkle* again. With five wins to her credit, she would now be an apprentice, or "bug," rider for one year.

All horses must carry a certain weight in order to race. This includes the jockey, equipment, and lead bars in the saddle. Apprentice riders, though, are allowed to carry less weight. This lets the horse run faster, so new jockeys get a chance to compete with the more experienced riders. The weight allowance is marked in the program by an asterisk that looks like a tiny bug. So, an apprentice rider is often called a "bug rider."

After she had been at the Tampa racetrack for a while, Julie met a young woman named Julie Snellings, who worked in the track officials' office. Julie Snellings watched every race on the closed circuit TV in her office. Julie Krone would sneak in there if she lost and ask the older woman what she had done wrong.

Julie Krone remembers one day when her friend gave her more advice than she felt she needed. "I hollered at her. 'If you know so much, why don't you ride?' Then she rolled out from behind the desk...in a wheelchair. I could feel my mouth drop open."

"Look, I've been a rider," Julie Snellings said.

"If you want to do better, then listen to me."

Julie did. She found out that her friend had been one of the best female riders on the Maryland/Delaware racing circuit in 1977. She had been paralyzed when a horse fell on her.

"Julie was the friend I needed at that stage in my life," Julie Snellings says. "I felt that I had nothing to live for. Then she came along: strong, tough, and talented."

Julie Snellings called her former agent in Maryland, Chick Lang, Jr. He agreed to be the young rider's agent. In fact, he offered to let her stay with his family until she could afford to live alone.

Maryland trainers did not want to work with Julie at first. Chick could only get her "longshots," horses with little chance of winning. Finally, after two weeks, Julie won with a horse named *Barbary Pirate.*

A Monmouth Park outrider leads Julie back to the winner's circle.

Certain that she was on her way to success, Julie was up before dawn every spring morning, stopping at all the barns around the track. She would say "good morning" to everyone, and offer doughnuts to the trainers. The people at the track were pleasant and friendly. Yet after two months, she had ridden only forty times and won only five races.

Things were not as friendly on the track. The other jockeys, who joked with her in the riders' room, sometimes tried to bump her or cut her off during races. Some of this was a part of horse racing, but much of it was their way to see how easy Julie was to scare.

Some days, Julie came off the track screaming, promising to punch the nose of the next person who bothered her. She was about ready to pack up and return to Michigan when she got a chance to ride for a well-known trainer, Bud Delp. He had many good horses in his stable.

Julie went with the Delp stable to Delaware Park. On July 1, nearly a year after her first race in Michigan, Julie won three races in a row. Within two weeks, she had a record of six days with either

Julie's racing style earned her a reputation as a daring rider. Here, she rides Forty-Niner *to victory.*

two or three winners each day. Julie was feeling very sure of herself, so she did what many other jockeys would never have done.

One morning, she went to talk to Julie Snellings, who had moved to work at the Delaware track and shared an apartment with Julie Krone. Delaware

Park was the track at which Julie Snellings had been injured. Julie Krone took her friend's old riding outfit from the closet and put it on. When she got to the track, she won three races wearing it. For Julie Snellings, the track's "bad luck" had been changed.

By the end of 1981, Julie had gained a reputation as a bold rider. She had moved to Maryland to work for trainer John Forbes. By this time, Julie was the top female bug rider in the world, but being a woman was still a drawback. The best male bug rider in Maryland still got more mounts than she did.

On February 26, 1982, Julie set a track record as the first female rider in Maryland to win four races in one day. Then her apprentice year was over. Julie knew that no woman had ever become famous in horse racing, yet that was what she planned to do.

Julie enjoys a relaxed moment during a workout ride.

Just keep riding and you always have a chance

In the months following the end of Julie's apprentice year, she didn't get many mounts. She felt it was because she was a female rider, and trainers still didn't trust her skills. Julie decided that the only way to be treated like a male jockey was to act like one. So she kept her hair short and wore no makeup or dresses. When she introduced herself to trainers, she shook their hands firmly to show her strength. She fought back tears and smiles—anything she thought might make her look weak.

Julie also decided to ride as roughly as some of the other riders on the track. This sometimes got her suspended for a few days. Yet no matter how hard she tried, Julie did not get the fast horses.

As the summer of 1982 neared, Julie moved to the New Jersey area and rode at the Atlantic City racetrack. There she met Larry Cooper, a determined young agent. He was able to get her more mounts, and she began to win.

Since Atlantic City was a night racing track, Julie often rode at nearby Monmouth Park in the afternoon. Her day began with workouts at dawn and often didn't end until midnight. Sometimes she rode in ten or twelve races each day. Despite the long hours, she enjoyed the hard work.

"Work, get me more work," she would tease Larry as he drove her from one track to another. Sometimes she would take a quick nap in the car.

By the end of the summer, Julie had become the first female rider to win the meeting, or racing season, at Atlantic City. She next moved to northern New Jersey to ride at The Meadowlands.

December night racing at The Meadowlands means warm gloves and a cold nose.

Peter Shannon (far left), *one of Julie's early supporters, poses with her in the winner's circle.*

Here she rode for trainer John Forbes and one of his biggest employers, Peter Shannon. Julie spent many hours at the Shannon home. "I remember the first night she came to dinner with our family," Peter says. "She was trying to act like a hot shot. 'Toss me a roll,' she said. So I did. She loved it!"

Julie won often at The Meadowlands. But if she lost, fans became angry with Peter and John. One day John Forbes got a letter from a fan asking, "Why do you use that girl?" Sometimes, Julie had to pass racing fans waiting for her on her way to the jockeys' quarters who shouted things such as, "Go home and wash the dishes!"

But Julie was not about to give up. At the beginning of 1983, Julie was feeling as if all her dreams were coming true. She was only nineteen years old, but she had her own apartment and had made new friends. She had won 155 races in 1982 and made more than $1 million in purse, or prize, money. Even though, as a jockey, she kept only 10 percent of her horses' winnings (in this case, about $100,000) and had to pay 25 percent of that to her agent, Julie felt rich.

She was also becoming famous. Several news-

As Julie became well known, loyal fans often asked for her auto-graph.

paper articles had been written about her and her riding career. She finally felt in control of her life.

Then track officials found some marijuana in her car. Julie was suspended from race riding for thirty days. If she repeated the crime, it could mean the loss of her jockey's license.

"It was pure torture," Julie remembers of those days. "I hadn't been off a horse for that long in seventeen years. But I'm glad it happened. It gave me a chance to think about the talent I had been given. I almost threw it away. I was young, but that was no excuse for being stupid."

Her first day back on the racetrack, Julie was nervous. "I thought the crowd would be angry with me, but they wished me good luck."

In October 1983, Julie rode a horse at New York's famous Belmont Park and won. It was her first victory at such an important track. Looking around the jockeys' room, she felt as though she were in a racing hall of fame for riders. Angel Cordero, one of the best-known jockeys there, paid her the highest compliment she could have received. "You don't ride like no girl jockey," he said.

That winter, Julie returned to Maryland to ride. One morning she was exercising a horse when the protective wrappings around his legs came loose. The horse tripped and fell, tossing Julie into the air and onto her back.

She lay on the track, unable to move her legs. "This is unbelievable," she remembers thinking. Thoughts of her friend Julie Snellings were in her mind all the way to the hospital. Luckily, the X rays showed a broken back, but no injury to the spinal cord. She wouldn't be paralyzed.

After a stay in the hospital, Julie had to wear an uncomfortable back brace. The worst pain came, though, when she looked in the newspaper each morning and saw other jockeys riding her horses.

She worked hard on her therapy, determined to get back to the track quickly. The doctors thought her recovery time of three months was a record!

By this time, John Forbes's stable had moved to Keystone, a racetrack near Philadelphia, Pennsylvania. Julie couldn't get good mounts, and she lost several of her first races. A long-time jockey told her, "If things aren't going your way, don't try to fix anything. Just keep riding and you'll always have a chance."

She soon had that chance. She and a midwest jockey, Patricia (PJ) Cooksey, were both invited to compete in a women's international jockey challenge series in Japan. Julie was able to ride against well-known riders from many countries.

Julie exercises a horse after recovering from her back injury.

Midway through the series, Julie came down with a fever of 105°F. The doctors at the hospital told her it was caused by an infection, which was a result of her former back injury.

While she was being treated, Julie made the nurses keep her sitting upright in bed. That way, she wouldn't feel dizzy when she rode again.

Finally, the doctors said she could race—on one condition. An ambulance drove her to the jockeys' room, and waited while she raced. Then it took her back to the hospital. Even with her illness, Julie managed to win five races.

It had been a year in which Julie's desire to be a jockey had been tested over and over again. She had proved that she could race with the best of them.

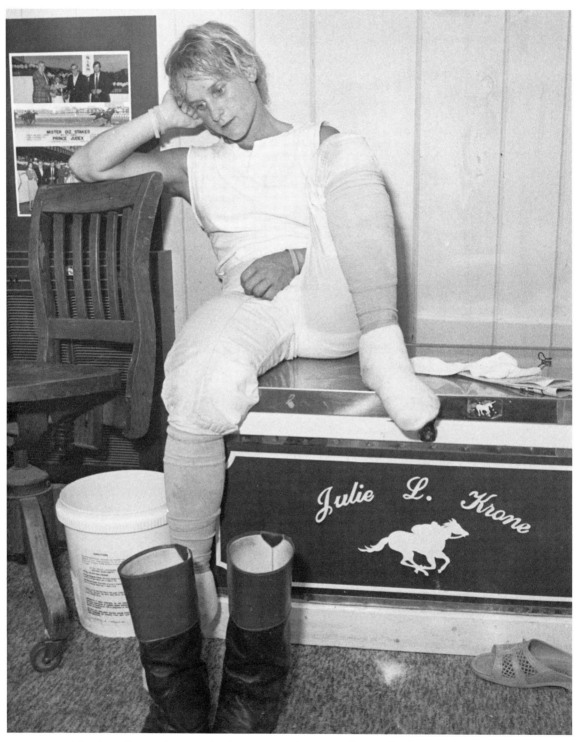

Moving from city to city is a normal part of a jockey's life. Here, a weary Julie rests on her trunk.

4

If you want a girl jockey, get somebody else

For the next two years, Julie moved many times, never staying in one place for very long. "Home is wherever I am," she says. She can't remember how many apartments and houses she has rented since she began her racing career. Sometimes she has to call information to get her phone number. No matter where she lives, though, Julie always has a cat or two to greet her when she gets home. She plans to have a dog, too, but not until she settles down.

Riding in several races a day keeps Julie very busy. Yet she does find time to read, and especially enjoys biographies of famous people.

In the spring of 1986, Julie moved again, this time to New Jersey's Garden State Park. She finally felt as if she was beginning to overcome what she calls the "male-female thing." The other jockeys no longer treated her as "just a girl."

Julie's spirits were high and she was looking forward to the move to Monmouth Park later that year. Then a call from her mother changed her whole life.

Julie had known that her mother, who had moved to Florida, had been ill. Doctors were doing surgery to find out what was wrong.

On the telephone, Judi told her daughter that the doctors had found abdominal cancer. They had given her only two years to live, even if she had surgery and radiation treatments.

Julie was stunned by the news. She couldn't understand how a woman as young as her mother could be sick enough to die. The thought of losing her mother's support frightened her.

As Judi Krone began to put all her energies into fighting the cancer, Julie worked even harder at riding. She rode every race as though her mother's life depended on it. Soon, she was winning two or three races each day.

"Call my mother and tell her I won," she would shout to whomever was near a phone. Then she would change into new riding silks and return to the track.

After her surgery, Judi moved to a lodge run by the hospital. She stayed there while she received radiation therapy. Julie sent videotapes of her races to Florida, and Judi watched them with the other patients.

"Those tapes kept me going," Judi says. "Julie's career gave me a reason to fight for life."

One day, Julie came home upset about dropping her whip on the track and losing the race. She called her mother to tell her. Before she could, though, Judi told her that the radiation was making her hair fall out. "That made me realize how unimportant my little problems were," Julie remembers.

Julie Krone's drive to win on the track gave her little time for people who still saw her as "that girl."

"If you want a *girl* jockey, get somebody else," she told them. "If you want a race rider, try me."

When 1986 ended, Julie had won 199 races and more than $2 million in purse money. On her last night at The Meadowlands, she set a new female record by winning four races. She spent Christmas visiting with her mother.

Julie's 1987 season at Monmouth Park in New Jersey seemed like one long victory to her. In August, she became only the third rider in the track's history to win six races in one day. At the end of the season, Julie had won fifty races more than any other jockey at the New Jersey track.

After winning the meeting at Monmouth, Julie moved to The Meadowlands once again. Here she would have a chance to race against her friend, Chris Antley. Chris had won the Monmouth Park title in 1984, 1985, and 1986, then moved to New York to race. Julie would have been even happier with her 1987 Monmouth title if he had been among the jockeys she had beaten.

"We have always had this love-hate relationship," Julie told a reporter. Off the track, they are close friends. Once they get on the track, though, "we try like crazy to beat each other," Julie says.

At The Meadowlands, Julie was riding in eight races a night and winning many of them. She decided it was time to try her luck in New York, too. If she was ever going to become well known in the "big leagues," she had to go there. Chris told her it

Julie poses with fellow jockey, Chris Antley.

would be like going from high school to college. She soon found out he was right. In New York, the purses were large, and jockeys were very serious about winning.

Julie finished the 1987 racing season at the head of The Meadowlands' jockey standings. She also set a women's record at Aqueduct, one of the New York racetracks, by winning four races on one day. Julie finished the year with a total of 324 wins, and was the sixth-leading jockey in the United States.

As her victories began to add up, Julie thought more and more about passing the record held by her friend, PJ Cooksey. PJ had 1,204 victories, and was the leading female jockey in the country. Julie had a chance at winning this title.

By February 29, 1988, Julie had won 1,199 races. She went to Garden State Park to see if she could win number 1,200 that night.

Julie is showered with champagne to celebrate her 1,205th win, making her the leading female jockey in the world.

In the eighth race of the evening, Julie had only one horse ahead of her. As she pulled alongside it, her horse's head suddenly jerked to the right. She lost her balance and her reins. Julie came in second, clinging to her horse's neck to keep from falling off.

The accident had happened so fast, Julie had not

known what had happened. The video replay showed that the jockey in the lead had pulled the reins from Julie's hands as she tried to pass him. The other jockey was suspended for six months, and Julie had won number 1,200.

On March 6, Julie had only one win to go to beat PJ Cooksey's record. With the long shadows of late afternoon falling on the track, Julie rode *Squawter* to the front of the pack and stayed there. She had set a new record!

When Julie got off her horse in the winner's circle, she noticed a lot of jockeys standing around waiting for her. Angel Cordero moved toward her, and the others followed. Suddenly, she was being showered with champagne. Soaked and shivering, Julie could never remember a bath feeling that good.

After finishing sixth at Aqueduct, Julie returned to The Meadowlands to capture the 1988 title there.

Helping the sport as well as myself

Julie finished the winter meeting at Aqueduct in sixth place. Her friend Chris Antley had come in first. Julie had learned so much by racing against top jockeys, though, that she didn't feel too bad about not beating Chris in New York.

Julie decided that she had done what she had set out to do—race and win in New York. She was now ready to listen to her friends and return to Monmouth Park to defend her 1987 title there. Before she went, an accident almost ruined her plans.

During the first race on Memorial Day at Belmont Park, Chris Antley's horse tripped and went down with Chris on him. A horse ridden by another of Julie's close friends, Richard Migliore, tried to jump the horse and rider, but failed. Richard was thrown from the horse. Julie's horse ran into the fallen horses, tossing her against the track's plastic railing.

All three horses got up. Julie struggled to her feet, too, but her two friends lay still on the ground. Both were taken to the hospital. Chris had a severe concussion, a type of head injury. Richard needed surgery for a broken spine.

For the first time in her career, Julie was afraid. She had only three days before the June 3 opening at Monmouth Park, and she wasn't sure if she could get back on a horse. Then she remembered her mother's words when she had fallen off Dixie: "You've got to get right back on."

In spite of her nervousness and the pain from the fall, Julie showed up at Monmouth Park and won four races on her first day at the track. Julie

Julie accepts an award for the 1988 Meadowlands riding title.

went on to win the 1988 Monmouth title. Next, she moved to The Meadowlands, hoping to win there, too. During the first part of that meeting, Julie and Chris Antley, who had recovered from his injuries, won almost the same number of races.

Midway through the meeting, though, Chris was

suspended for using drugs. When she heard, Julie called to tell him that getting caught and punished was the best thing that could have happened. He would return to the track a better person.

One of Julie's biggest thrills came in November 1988 when she rode on Breeders' Cup Day. No woman had ever taken part in those races before. The Breeders' Cup is an afternoon of racing in which every race is worth $1 million, and the feature race is worth $3 million. Although she didn't win that day, Julie felt honored to be racing with some of the world's best jockeys.

The Breeders' Cup Race had been held at Churchill Downs, Kentucky, that year. People from Julie's home town had come to see her ride. She was happiest to see her mother. The doctors said the cancer was in remission, which meant Judi no longer had any of the disease's symptoms.

In 1988, Julie was the first woman to ride in the Breeders' Cup races, contests between the best horses and the best jockeys in the world.

Julie finished 1988 as the fourth leading rider in the United States. She began 1989 with the same energy, becoming the leading jockey in New York. She set a new record as the first female to win five races in one day.

Then in February, Julie went to the White

House to meet President George Bush. She had been chosen as one of eight female athletes to be honored on National Women in Sports Day.

Many articles have been written about Julie since she first started winning races. At first, Julie says, "all the attention was flattering. After a while, though, I started thinking—not again."

Jockeys such as Angel Cordero have helped her deal with fame. Although Angel has won more than six thousand races and is a member of the Racing Hall of Fame, he took an interest in Julie and her career. He showed her not only how to improve her riding, but also how to handle the many reporters wanting to interview her. "I had to learn to separate my personal life from my career," she says. She also learned she is a spokesperson for thoroughbred racing. "I have to concentrate on helping the sport as well as myself."

President George Bush honors Julie Krone on National Women in Sports Day.

Julie has appeared on television programs such as "The Tonight Show" and "Late Night with David Letterman." Her story has been featured in *Sports Illustrated*, *Newsweek*, and *People*, as well as all the major horse racing magazines.

Usually the reporting is correct. One night,

though, Julie was listening to the nightly news when a sports broadcaster said that she had fallen and broken an arm and a leg. Luckily, he was wrong. She had fallen off a horse and was badly bruised, but she mended quickly and was soon back at the track.

All the honors Julie has received have made her happy, but a little uncomfortable. Everyone has told her how well she has done. Yet she can't help but think they still mean "as a woman."

In June 1989, Julie moved again. This time, she went to Monmouth Park, where she won the riding title for the third straight year. Julie is not sure when she will stop moving around—"maybe ten years." Her racing career has made it hard for her to get to know people well.

Yet she says she does have a boyfriend, and would like to have a family someday. She would also like to have a farm for her children to enjoy as she did when she was growing up, perhaps in Colorado.

Julie knows that horse racing is a sport in which fame can disappear quickly. "You have to set new goals everyday," she has often said. Her goals include riding the fastest horses in the fastest races. She would one day like to be able to ride in the Triple Crown races—the Kentucky Derby, the Preakness, and the Belmont.

But she knows she must first work harder to erase the word *female* from comments about her riding.

"I don't want to be the best female jockey in the world," she says. "I want to be the best jockey."

GLOSSARY

apprentice—a rider who is in his or her first year as a jockey

Arabian—the oldest pure breed of horse, found as far back as 5000 B.C. on the Arabian peninsula; ancestor of the thoroughbred in England

dressage—a series of precision steps a horse is trained to perform, showing rhythm, balance, and stride. For example, the horse is taught to walk in circles, lines, or figure eights

half-mile pole—a striped marker indicating a half-mile distance to the finish line

meeting—a specific number of days during which racing is held at a particular track

mount—the horse a jockey rides in a race

purse—money given to the owner of a winning horse. In the early days of racing, owners would each put their "stakes" in a purse which the winner received

racing silks—multi-colored shirts worn by jockeys in colors and designs registered to the owner of the horse they will ride

reins—leather straps attached to horse's headpiece (bridle) used to guide the horse in different directions

show jumping—competition in which horses jump fences for speed and accuracy

starting gate—a moveable, electronic enclosure into which horses are led before a race. Gates in front of the horses spring open at the same time to allow them an even start

trail riding—a timed competition over a trail

winner's circle—the area in front of the grandstand where a winning horse is brought after the race

INDEX